the MAINE COON CAT

Liza Gardner Walsh

Down East Books

Photographs courtesy of: Andy Barron: 35; Jeannie Brett: 80, 81; Don Carrigan, 71-73, 75; Mary Cassatt (*Sarah Holding a Cat,* 1908), 86; Lynda Chilton, 8; Dreamstime, 6, 7, 11, 13-16, 18, 24, 27-28, 33, 36, 38, 44-45, 56, 60, 62-63, 65-66, 70, 87-88, 90; Fotolia, 11, 12, 14, 21, 22, 23, 45, 47, 51, 58, 82-83; Istock, 3, 14, 19, 48-49, 57; Lynn Karlin, 5, 10, 20, 29, 84; Beth Kus/Dirigo, 11, 46, 91, 93; Kimberly Lockie: 64; Collections of Maine Historical Society: 42; Dave Menke: 26; Martin van Meytens (*Marie Antoinette at Age 13,* 1767), 30; Oleg Morgan, 67; Jean-Babtiste Perronneau (*Girl with a Kitten*), 30; Pussy's Port o' Call: 54; Barrie Pribyl: 79; Pierre-Auguste Renoir (*Woman with Cat* c.1875), 94; Sage Ross: 71; Hillary Steinau, 37, 52-53, 67; Barry Won, 68

ISBN 978-160893-250-4

Design by Lynda Chilton

Printed in the United States

Down East Books

A member of the Rowman & Littlefield Publishing Group

4501 Forbes Boulevard, Suite 200

Lanham, Maryland 20706

www.downeastbooks.com

Distributed by

NATIONAL BOOK NETWORK

1-800-462-6420

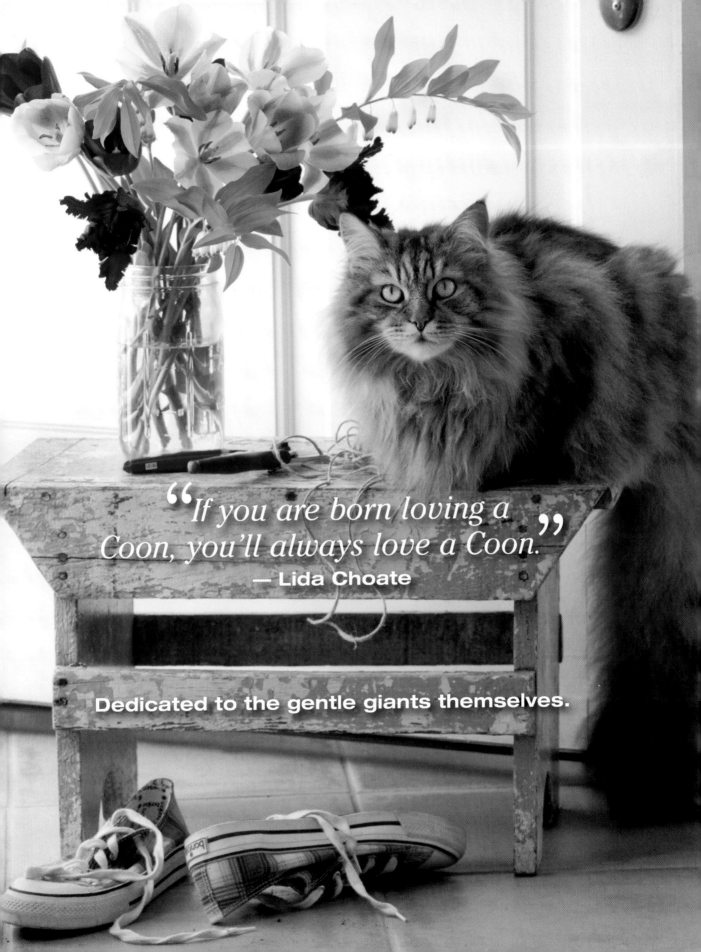

> *"If you are born loving a Coon, you'll always love a Coon."*
> — Lida Choate

Dedicated to the gentle giants themselves.

the CONTENTS

what is A MAINE COON CAT?

Physical Characteristics

" Of all cat breeds, the Maine Coon is probably the most complete package. After all, while not every person agrees on what makes another *person* beautiful, there is usually agreement as to the presence of charm, appeal, and charisma. And the Maine Coon, the genuine article, has it. **"**

— Marilis Hornidge, *That Yankee Cat*

The package that sets the Maine Coon apart, making it at once desirable and distinguished, has also made it rise in the ranks to become the second most popular cat, following closely behind the Persian. The cat's origins are a mystery — its genes tumbled in the salt spray of Maine's rugged coast and married with the genes of sea captains' cats from around the world until a perfectly adapted specimen evolved with its own unique attributes. These wild remnants are what is so intriguing about the breed, giving an appearance reminiscent of a bobcat or lynx. This untamed visage of the Maine Coon parallels the rustic state from where it hails. Put the cat and the state together and you have an enduring mystique. Perhaps that is why in 1985 the Maine Coon became Maine's official state cat, making it the only true cat breed in the country to serve in this honorable role.

Even those only remotely familiar with the breed have heard legends of their grand size — they are as big as the state of their origin.

Some are even huge, as breeders have, unfortunately, bred to suit people's fascination with gigantism in the breed. The large size of the cat, however, is disputed by Maine Coon expert and enthusiast Sharyn Bass, who attests, "the belief that a Maine Coon cat should weigh between thirty and forty pounds is stretching the imagination." She adds that in the past Maine Coons needed to be large for survival, but for today as a house pet, this "super giant" status is not necessary. A normal Maine Coon male weighs twelve to fifteen pounds, while a female weighs ten to twelve pounds. Often the Maine Coon is significantly larger than a small dog, its size exaggerated by its voluminous coat and fluffy tail.

Despite their size, Maine Coons develop slowly. The maturation process for a Maine Coon takes anywhere from three to five years, so for those who relish the youthful exuberance of a kitten, this breed is a perfect choice. As kittens, they grow quickly before slowing between four and eight months. They are even said to begin to walk, climb, and sometimes open their eyes earlier than kittens of other breeds.

An ample coat is another well-known attribute of the breed, but the coat of a Maine Coon is different from its long-haired brethren. Shaggy and uneven are two words often used to describe the coat, but in her book *That Yankee Cat,* Marilis Hornidge says it more elegantly: "The coat is like a custom-fitted garment with a lustrous sheen as if made of antique satin." But the coat is far more practical than satin as it is 100 percent water repellent, perfect for cold winters. Writer Mary L. Daniels adds, "It is decidedly strokeable, like liquid silk to the touch." Daniels cites a poll in which sixty-five percent of British cat owners confess they would rather cuddle their cats than their mates, and she believes that if they were petting Maine Coons, the statistic would be much higher.

The hindquarters of the Maine Coon are heavily furred and look like old-fashion pantaloons. The hair on the shoulders is shorter than the rest of the coat, making for a distinguished-looking Elizabethan ruff around the neck and chest. This coat evolved for the Maine Coon to survive in the rugged woods. According to Sharyn Bass, "The short hair on the shoulders, which only gets longer on the back and sides, enables cats to move through wooded areas without becoming entangled in trees and brambles. If the coat was the texture and length of a Persian, for example, the cat could have been easily trapped in briars and woods, unable to escape."

Tufts of fur rise out of the inside and tips of the Maine Coon's ears. In some enthusiasts' circles, these are called "lynx-tips." Hornidge notes, "The tufts on the tops and tips of the ears, almost vestigial in some and so heavy as to be reminiscent of the lynx and bobcat in others, are a genetic puzzle to breeders and an enchantment to photographers. They add another grace note from the wild and times past to the Maine Coon's appearance." As an evolutionary development, this feature adds more than warmth and "grace notes." Wild cats depend on their remarkable hearing ability and the large tufts allow sound to be absorbed from many angles.

The Maine Coon is known for its large, heavily tufted, snowshoe paws. These insulated booties are another adaptive trait for surviving winter. Maine Coons are surprisingly adept at maneuvering with their seemingly cumbersome digits and can carefully lift tiny items in the palm of their paw. These paws can be polydactyl, a trait that is not allowable in a show cat but one that is dear to the hearts of Maine Coon aficionados. This genetic mutation was encouraged in New England and has given rise to a rather large fleet of many-toed Coons. A normal-toed cat has a total of eighteen toes — five each on the front paws and four on the back. Polydactyl cats can have anywhere from four to seven toes per paw. Polydactylism is most common on the front paws. Ernest Hemingway became a lover of polydactyl cats after he was given one by a ship captain. Because of his ardent adoration, polydactyls are often called "Hemingway Cats."

The dramatic flourish of a Maine Coon's tail is its pride and joy, making them known as the tail with the cat attached. The fluffy tail is perfect for winter living, for who wouldn't want that feathery whorl wrapped around them in a snowstorm? Often ringed and proudly held upright, the tail is reminiscent of a raccoon's. Writer and Maine Coon enthusiast Diane Morgan remarks that, "Of course, it's scientifically impossible for raccoons or bobcats to mate with domestic cats. But having lived in Maine for many years, owned Maine Coons, and being well aware of the ways of bobcat and raccoon, I wonder. I wonder if the qualities of these mysterious and beautiful animals somehow, by some strange spiritual osmosis, entered the soul of this domestic cat and changed it forever."

This idea of "wild osmosis" is also expressed in the intensity of the Maine Coon's eyes, which are reminiscent of an owl peering at you, round and perfectly angled. The colors vary from green to gold to copper, with occasional blue eyes or off eyes (eyes of two different colors). The eyes are set into a squarish countenance that is a marker of the breed. This distinct head shape is what differentiates a Maine Coon from other long-haired cats. According to Hornidge, "It can have a feral, half-wild look, given by a nose with the characteristic that the fancy terms 'straightness.' This straightness is . . . a gentle in-curve from the forehead to the point at which the nose leaves the face and straight from there on. There is further a squareness to the muzzle, which is indeed referred to as a muzzle. Most cats have noses, but muzzle is the right word for the Maine Coon's, carrying as it does a connotation of the wild." The

Maine Coon has a large bone structure and an elongated rectangular body, unlike the more stocky and squarish build of Persians or other long-hair mixes.

The Colors of the Coon

The Maine Coon cat will never disappoint in its colorful finery. The lustrous coat seems designed to shimmer in nearly all varieties of cat color pattern except the pointed Himalayan and Siamese. A litter of Maine Coons might produce several different patterns of kittens, and the color names read like a list of poetry — smoke, cameo, cream, Maltese, mackerel, tortoiseshell.

Black and red are the two primary colors in cats and the mix of these dominant shades creates all of the resulting color variations. White plays an interesting role as it is a "masking gene," meaning it hides all other colors. A pure white cat is actually a red or a black but the color is masked by the dominant white gene. When a cat has white spots, it is termed "white spotting," which only masks some of the cat's color.

The International Cat Association has a list of official color and pattern names, but each term also has several common names. The following list of official colors and their common names was compiled by Beth Hicks, an all-breed judge with The International Cat Association. To learn about the specifics of color crossing and what colors cats can carry, the TICA Web site *(tica.org)* is an incredible resource.

Official Color	Commonly Called
Red	Orange, Rust, Marmalade, Yellow, Ginger
Blue	Gray, Grey
Chocolate	Brown
Seal	Brown
Silver	Grey or Gray
Black Tortie & White	Calico
Cream	Buff

As for patterns, they are: solid, tabby, torty, torby, and particolor. Many have come to recognize the Maine Coon as a traditional tabby, but within the tabby design there are four distinct patterns. Tabby is a dominant gene, which is why it seems so ever-present in cats. A tabby variation called "mackerel" consists of stripes all over the body with a connecting line running down the cat's spine. A tortoiseshell is a basic black cat with large patches of red and cream. This pattern can often have a "blaze," in which the face is evenly divided with black and one of the other colors represented on the body. A torty (tortoiseshell) with white will generally have white paws, bib, and belly, whereas a torby is a variant of the tortoiseshell with stripes instead of patches. For the most part, torties and torbies tend to be females. The term "smoke" is used to indicate that the cat has white mixed in and, as Hornidge describes, "the cat looks bleached, rather like the patina and shade acquired by old denim." If white is added to any of the above, the designation is termed particolor.

As different genes are modified, surprising color combinations can occur. Certain breeders find a color combination that they are particularly fond of and they fine-tune this tint over their entire careers. Playing with color in breeding is one of the most interesting genetic puzzles since the Maine Coon's palette is like an artist's box of paints. But the one color that is not represented is turquoise, despite the legend of the turquoise kitten. This myth is attached to the arrival of Marie Antoinette's cats to Maine (see p. 30), which were assumed to be Turkish Angoras. In French, the translation of Turkish is Turquis and at the time of their arrival, Maine and northern New England were home to many French speakers. The story goes that a French-speaking breeder of these long-haired kittens called them Turquis kittens without translating the name. Unassuming summer cat shoppers thought of their cats as a turquoise breed. As you will note from the exhaustive list of accepted Maine Coon cat colors, turquoise is definitely not listed!

The Amazing Technicolor Dream Cat

The following colors are acceptable in a show cat:

Blue Eyed White

Bluecream

Blue Tabby Particolor

Copper Eyed White

Tortoiseshell

Blue Silver Tabby Particolor

Odd Eyed White

Cream Tabby Particolor

Blue

Blue Smoke

Red Tabby Particolor

Black

Black Smoke

Brown Tabby Particolor

Cream

Cameo Smoke

Silver Tabby Particolor

Red

Golden Smoke

Golden Tabby

Particolor

Bluecream Smoke

Cameo Tabby

Particolor

Blue Tabby

Tortoiseshell Smoke

Blue McTabby Particolor

Blue Silver Tabby

Blue Silver McTabby Particolor

Cream Tabby

Chinchilla Silver

Cream McTabby Particolor

Red Tabby

Shaded Silver

Red McTabby Particolor

Brown Tabby

Shell Cameo

Brown McTabby Particolor

Silver Tabby

Shaded Cameo

Silver McTabby Particolor

Golden Tabby

Chinchilla Golden

Golden McTabby Particolor

Cameo Tabby

Shaded Golden

Cameo McTabby Particolor

Blue McTabby

Shaded Bluecream

Bluecream Particolor

Blue Silver McTabby

Shaded Tortoiseshell

Shaded Bluecream Particolor

Cream McTabby

Smoke Bluecream Particolor

Red McTabby

Blue Bicolor

Tortoiseshell Particolor

Brown McTabby

Black Bicolor

Shaded Tortoiseshell Particolor

Silver McTabby

Cream Bicolor

Smoke Tortoiseshell Particolor

Golden McTabby

Red Bicolor

Blue Patched Tabby Particolor

Cameo McTabby

Blue Silver Patched

Tabby Particolor

Blue Patched Tabby

Brown Patched Tabby Particolor

Blue Silver Patched Tabby

Silver Patched Tabby Particolor

Brown Patched Tabby

Golden Patched Tabby Particolor

Silver Patched Tabby

Blue Patched McTabby Particolor

Golden Patched Tabby

Blue Silver Patched

McTabby Particolor

Blue Patched McTabby

Brown Patched

McTabby Particolor

Blue Silver Patched McTabby

Silver Patched McTabby Particolor

Brown Patched McTabby

Golden Patched McTabby Particolor

Silver Patched McTabby

Golden Patched McTabby

Source: The American Association of Cat Enthusiasts

Temperament

There is little debate about why the Maine Coon hovers at the top of the cat popularity charts. Clearly, it is the seamless combination of striking good looks with a distinctive and charming personality. The unique temperament, colorful stories, and quirks that make up the interior world of the Maine Coon cat could fill volumes. The sight of a Maine Coon and the stories about them make people relaxed and nostalgic. They are not haughty, or overly aloof, in fact these cats often play and have a distinct sense of humor. As one breeder declared, they are "dignified but not pompous; demonstrative but not gushy; definite but not excessive." Maine Coons are affectionately known as the "gentle giants of the cat world." There is the oft-described dog-like trait, which is the combination of loyalty mixed with the willingness to endure a leash and take a stroll if necessary, the ability to be your best friend, and to even learn a few tricks. Writer Diane Morgan gives this description: "The Maine Coon is loyal and friendly, but not neurotically clingy. This easygoing, tranquil breed will not frazzle your nerves with ceaseless tearing around the house. Probably due to its working heritage, the Maine Coon knows when to dig in and when to take it easy. It's neither lazy nor an energy waster. Most enjoy a good romp early in the morning and again in the evening. The rest of the time they take it easy, like the sensible creatures they are."

Talking to any owner of a Maine Coon will immediately alert you to the quirks of the breed, with their renowned water fetish rising to the top. Many know how to turn on the faucets in their houses and will play with the streams of water for hours. Others are content to simply splash around in their water bowls, sliding them across the floor and tipping them over. Stories abound of Maine Coons napping in empty bathtubs and sinks and resting on the rims of bathtubs while their owners bathe.

Another strange quirk is the Maine Coon head butt. Yes, they like to charge with their heads, goat style, and literally butt into you. Those large, perfectly shaped heads become missile-like if you don't watch out. The Maine Coon is also fond of rising on its haunches to study something interesting.

The vocalizations of the Maine Coon are another peculiarity. The bird-like cheep and odd trills vary from the standard meow most cats are known for. Often, it sounds as if they are humming or muttering under their breath. One Maine Coon enthusiast has hypothesized that the larger the Maine Coon the smaller their voice.

The personalities of the Maine Coon vary depending upon gender. Some say the females appear more dignified while the males are more goofy and playful. There is also a sense that the females tend to covet the entire family while the male selects one person to favor and is indifferent to the rest of the brood. Marilis Hornidge wrote of the premier difference between the sexes: "Females are full of charm and affection with an implacable, quiet determination to have their own way, whereas the males are little boys and if cast into human form would have frogs in their pockets, freckles and dirt on their faces, and complete confidence that the world revolves around them." One thing is clear, the Maine Coon cat is not your run-of-the-mill cat. They are large in both personality and stature and they have made an even larger impact on the cat world.

Cool Facts About Coon Cats

Everyone knows the Maine Coon is big and beautiful, but there's more to this popular cat than that.

They float

Maine Coons are impressive, but though they can't walk on water they do have water-resistant fur that allows them to withstand harsh frigid climates and lets them swim almost effortlessly through water.

They can handle the cold

Maine Coons have long, bushy tails that are very pretty. They're also practical as they can be used to keep the cat's face and shoulders warm in the snow and cold.

They can handle the snow

They are also called snowshoe cats for the big tufts of fur between their toes that work like built-in snowshoes and help prevent them from sinking into deep snow.

They're super smart

Maine Coons are very intelligent, affectionate, and loyal. They have been called doglike for their ability to learn tricks — they can be taught to play fetch and walk on a leash — and for their devotion to their owners. They also have a wide range of vocalizations and some are said to actually sing.

They love to play

Coon cats take longer to mature than other cats. Perhaps it's this added time as a kitten that makes them so playful — they especially love to play in water. They are often called "gentle giants" because they are so easygoing. Coon cats are sociable and can handle both calm and active households.

the cat of
A HUNDRED TALES

" Around the origins of the Maine Coon cat swirls a fog of legend and conjecture as the fogs of its homeland. There is a wealth of romantic tradition, of genetic theory, of natural-selection stories, so broad and colorful as to be the envy of any other breed. There are dashing sea captains, Mendelian theorists and cracker-barrel P.T. Barnums. None of these tales, be they scrubbed theory or embellished legend, can be proved so conclusively as to eliminate the others. Each has its partisan backers willing to take up the verbal cudgels in defense of their pet theory. **"**

— Marilis Hornidge, *That Yankee Cat*

Man had no direct hand in the evolution of America's only natural breed of domestic cat, so instead a million stories are told to explain how the Maine Coon came to be. The stories are as colorful as the cat on which they are based, but no one knows the exact truth — as Marilis Hornidge aptly puts it: "The only ones who know for sure are the Maine Coon and the Great Pattern Maker in the sky. And they aren't telling." So cat enthusiasts are left to wonder and spin their delicious tales. Many have heard of the fabulous link between Marie Antoinette's royal cats merging to create the Maine Coon, while others fancy the impossible idea of a marriage between a raccoon and domestic cat. When all the stories are laid out on the table like a giant puzzle, the pieces form a whole — the evolution of a breed made up of imported seafaring cats living in a harsh climate, resulting in a naturally selected feline beauty.

The Maine Coon and the Raccoon

L et's get this one out of the way first. Yes, the Maine Coon cat has a big, fluffy, and sometimes ringed tail that it often holds upright for long periods of time. And it does enjoy a view from its haunches like a raccoon. But it is a terrific impossibility for a raccoon and a cat to mate. Science does not allow for the mating of two different species. More specifically, the parts don't fit and thus a raccoon-cat baby could not be created. The life of this story was extended by a conversation recorded in the 1937 Maine Writer's Project, when a local declared that the breed originated when a cat from China, Maine, mated with a raccoon.

Raccoon

But you can't deny that the two creatures do indeed share a name. Many theories abound on the origin of this name choice. Some say a farm wife remarked that the cat looked like a raccoon due to its tail, and so the cats alternated between the name coon cats and shags. They were also simply known as Maine cats. A legend originating from the Biddeford Pool area of Maine concerns a Captain Coon, who is perhaps the namesake of the breed. According to breeder Lida Choate, the story goes that "a cabin boy named Tom Coon collected cats while ashore to rid the sailing vessel he worked on of wharf rats. On one of these rat-catcher expeditions in a foreign land, Tom snuck in a beautiful longhair. The safe harbor for the first coon and her subsequent litter was the Tarbox Farm at Biddeford Pool, where the boy's ship anchored to take on supplies. When the cabin boy became a captain, he continued to bring the exotic long-hairs to the farm during his ocean voyages."

Marilis Hornidge's version of this story differs a little in that Captain Coon traversed the eastern seaboard with his herd of exotic cats, and whenever he landed, his cats disembarked, including a striking pack of long-hairs, who went visiting, as cats often do. After Captain Coon set sail again, long-haired kittens began appearing in local litters and the common utterance was, "One of Coon's cats, again."

The Bobcat Marriage

Bobcat

The wild look of the Maine Coon, with its lynx-tip ears and feral muzzle, are enough for some to give credence to the theory of the union between the bobcat and the domestic feline. Apparently there exist documented eyewitness accounts from Texas in 1949 and North Dakota in 1954 of matings between domestic and wild cats producing viable offspring. The prevalence of bobcats in the New England region is another tip on the scale for this theory. Still, many scientists doubt this merging could occur for the same reasons as the raccoon theory. And many of the bobcat-like features on the Maine Coon could simply be a result of naturally selected traits needed for survival in a harsh climate. But for those who cherish the wildness and untamed countenance of their Maine Coon cat, this theory of a strapping bobcat ancestor gives their own cat a connection to the wild.

Marie Antoinette

Just as invoking the majesty of the mighty bobcat excites some, others feel a rush from thinking about the royal connection of their cat to France's last queen. One of the most quixotic of the Maine Coon origin tales is the link between Marie Antoinette's royal cats and Captain Samuel Clough of Wiscasset, Maine. As with most things in life, two camps are divided in this tale, the romantics and the realists. To the romantics, Captain Clough saw Marie Antoinette as the ultimate damsel in distress. So committed to saving the queen was Clough that he endangered his crew by loading their vessel with the queen's personal effects, including six of her fluffy long-haired cats. He even put his home life in peril, writing his wife to prepare their house for the queen to take residence with them. The romantics would certainly adore this re-imagined story created by Maude Clark Gay in 1919 and told from the point of view of

his daughter, Rosalind. This story, "The Legend of Rosalind," imagines Captain Clough's journey, gushing his tender concern for the wronged queen and his desperation to free her. Alas, he is only able to return with her belongings and they are placed in the residence prepared for her — fading to rags or carried off by souvenir hunters over the years. The queen lives on, however, in young Rosalind, who grows up hearing stories of the ill-fated queen and even names her own daughter Antoinette.

This period painting shows a young girl perhaps Rosalind Clough's age holding what appears to be a Maine Coon kitten.

Counter to this fabulously textured tale, the realists contend that Captain Clough was a Yankee, meaning that he was "practical, hard-headed, and adventurous only if well-paid." When it seemed as if Marie Antoinette would be unable to complete her payment due to her jail sentence and date with the guillotine, hovering in port loaded with the queen's possessions, and

Above: Wiscasset in Marie Antoinette's day.
Left: The house in Wiscasset where Antoinette would have come to live.

faced with the possibility of execution himself, the sensible captain hightailed the schooner for home. According to both legends, the ship was filled to the brim with furniture, cloth, wallpaper, china, silver, and, most importantly, the queen's cats. It is these six royal cats that the story rests on, for when they reached the shores of Maine and met the local cats, they spread their majestic genes to the kittens, which became the noble ancestors of the Maine Coon cat.

The Vikings

The snow-covered northern climes of Scandinavia are not so different, if a tad more extreme, than the rugged terrain of Maine, so the theory of the Vikings bringing early descendants of the Maine Coon on their extensive

Norwegian Skogkatt or Forest Cat

seafaring expeditions to the east coast of North America in 1000 AD is a fairly logical origin tale. The cats of Scandinavia are very similar to the Maine Coon and according to an off-the-record comment by a judge at a Berlin cat show, are basically the same breed. The Norwegian Skogkatt, Danish Racekatt, and Swedish Rugkatt all share traits with its American cousin, the Maine Coon. One of the specific shared traits is their hunting prowess. Why wouldn't a no-nonsense Viking pack a cat on board for the same reasons that later sea captains did, to protect the grain stores from rodent infestation? And just as those later feline stowaways met the local port cats, who is to say the Scandinavians didn't leave a few kittens behind in the new world to rough it and form the foundation for the Maine Coon?

There is also a speculative connection between Marie Antoinette and the Swedish Rugkatt. Marie Antoinette's notorious paramour was the Swedish Diplomat and French Royalist Count Axel Von Fersen. His renowned devotion to the queen may have prompted him to bring her one of the prized long-haired cats from his homeland, as she was known for her love of furry pets. Thus, those same famous cats that sailed on Captain Clough's schooner might also have been tied to these northern relations.

Evolution and the Coastal Connection

However the first Maine Coon ancestors arrived, whether on a Viking dragon ship or by mixing with the wild bobcat, the most rational and logical theory is what Marilis Hornidge calls the "you-don't-fool-mother-nature-theory." She continues, "It is much more delightful to think that Marie Antoinette rode to the guillotine reassured that her cats would have a good home, or to picture Leif Ericson with a furry kitten perched on his shoulder, or even to imagine the raw-sex wilderness encounter of the domestic puss with the noble savage." But

the most likely theory is that these amazing creatures were formed by the slow melding of genes, and their characteristic traits are the Darwinian adaptations needed to thrive in a particular climate. The Maine coast was the choice place for sea captains to reside and as they settled along the shore, they brought their beloved and respected cats to live with them. In the following passage, Maine Coon breeder Beth Kus discusses this maritime genetic pool that shaped the Maine Coons:

"Two hundred years ago, and even now, the Maine harbor villages were isolated and the cat population was small. These few early cats were nurtured and allowed to multiply until they naturally bred true to type in this magical location, with the beautiful sea, family farms, and harborside villages set in this cold northern climate. The breed could not have developed in Boston, for example, because there would have been too many other cats to dilute the gene pool. The Boston influence, however, can be seen in the polydactyl Maine Coons that still naturally occur."

Fallacies and Urban Legends

One of the most legendary folktales surrounding the Maine Coon comes from the Revolutionary War era and concerns a certain "shag" who saved a family from starvation. The father was off fighting in the war and supplies in the house were sparse, but their loyal cat replenished the stores by bringing home "ice fish" each day from an open spot in the river. During the height of sea travel, coon cats were known for their uncanny abilities to call the wind or to calm it, making them a good-luck token on many sea voyages. There are even ghost stories about dead coon cats that return to their favorite spots, and coons that save their owners' lives by sensing impending doom.

But it is the size of the Maine Coon that has generated more than its share of stories, and some are so grand that you can't help cracking a smile at their absurdity. Two such fabulous stories were run by tabloids; one in *The Examiner* told of giant Maine Coons "bred for size and ferocity by unscrupulous breeders, terrorizing lonely farms and towns in New England." The other story, run by *The Daily Mirror* of London, describes "a large domestic cat called 'Coonmain' which was rampaging through the suburbs of Edgeware."

A few years ago, a Photoshopped image of a man holding a Maine Coon the size of a Rottweiler circled the Internet. A fabricated story went along with the hoax: A fictional character named Rodger Degagne lived in Canada and worked at a nuclear research facility. Rodger recounts finding two stray cats while on his lunch break at the nuclear facility. Tempting them with a tuna sandwich, he brought them home and named them Lost and Found. The two cats mated and the kitten they kept became the giant known in the cyber world as "Snowball." According to Rodger, "Snowball literally snowballed," growing to sixty-nine inches and

A cat by any other name . . .
Some alternative names for the Maine Coon Cat

American Longhair
Coon Cat
Maine Cat
Maine Shag
Snowshoe Cat
Yankee Cat

In 2006, the Guinness World Records named a male purebred Maine Coon the "Longest Cat." Verismo Leonetti Reserve Red (better known as Leo) measured 48 inches (120cm) in length, from the tip of his nose to the tip of his tail, and weighed 35 pounds (16kg). That record was broken in 2010 by another Maine Coon. A male purebred named Stewie measured 48.5 inches (123cm) from nose to tail.

Stewie

eighty-seven pounds. Snowball ate whole cooked chickens, scared away German shepherds, and the Degagnes supposedly even found a half-eaten raccoon. When questioned about how Snowball got so big, Rodger said, "Well, the vet thinks it could be her thyroid, but she isn't fat, she's just a real big cat. I think maybe her parents got into something at the nuclear plant that they shouldn't have."

The real story behind "Snowball," is much less explosive. A man named Cordell Hauglie simply Photoshopped a picture of him holding his cat Jumper as a joke for his daughter. He emailed it to some of his friends and forgot all about it until the story began to make the rounds. Hauglie certainly had no intention of creating such a giant hoax. 🐈

the rise, fall, and rise again of the
MAINE COON CAT

History of the Breed

The Maine Coon is the only natural American breed of cat. Yet the breed's popularity cycled through a myriad of changes between their heyday in the late nineteenth century through today. In fact, the Maine Coon's development as a distinct breed looks like an upside-down bell curve. Wildly popular, then completely forgotten, then back to the top of the charts. Maine Coons were among the first to be shown in the 1800s but, ironically, were not admitted in those same show halls later in the twentieth century.

At the first Skowhegan Fair in the 1860s, the Maine Coon competed for Maine State Champion Coon Cat, making this the first cat show exclusively designated for a single breed. All sources prove that Maine Coons were shown long before the popularity of cat shows took off, both at home and abroad. During the Victorian Age, the Maine Coon siezed hold of the cat fancy and rode it to the top, becoming a renowned show cat and a desirable pet. The Maine Coon was "a class unto itself." At a Boston Cat Show in 1878, twelve Maine Coons were shown. In 1895, at the first national cat show, held at Madison Square Garden, first place and best in show went to Cosey, a Maine Coon brown tabby female. This was the beginning of what is known as "show fever" and the Maine Coons regally rode the wave

NATIONAL CAT SHOW 1895 WON BY COSEY.

The Saturday Evening Post ran an article in 1901 entitled "Backyard Business Enterprises: Raising Cats for Profit." The article discussed the

rearing of Coon cats and the boom of exporting this precious cargo. At that time, Maine Coon cats sold for anywhere between five dollars and one hundred dollars, with "exceptional specimens fetching two or three hundred dollars." The author states that, "at the present time all of them come from Maine, simply for the reason that the breed is particular as yet to that state. Their popularity is such that the business of breeding them has been rapidly growing during the last few years in that part of the country, and one shipper not very far from Bar Harbor, exported in 1899 no fewer than three thousand of the animals." This gross exportation of the breed during the early twentieth century is thought to have greatly depleted the population.

In the renowned *Book of the Cat* by Frances Simpson, published in 1903, there is an entire chapter devoted to "Maine Cats." The author of this chapter, Mrs. F.R. Pierce, claims the first Maine Coon on record with the weighty name of Captain Jenks of the Horse Marines. This chapter clearly portrays "Maine Cats" as a desired and distinctive breed in their own right. At a Portland Cat Show in 1911, with one hundred seventy entries, a Maine Coon took home the grand prize, the last big win for the cat for the next forty years. "After such an auspicious beginning, snobbery began to raise its ugly head. As cats and their breeding began to attract more and more interest countrywide, the improved breeds became status symbols," said author Marilis Hornidge.

Over the tumultuous four decades to follow, those few Maine Coons still left in the state after their frenzied exodus were highly prized by their Maine families and performed faithful porch duty. As a breed they were tossed aside by the popularity of other exotic imports, but several Maine Coon enthusiasts kept diligent records and didn't let the breed fall into a feline abyss. The breed was championed by the Central Maine Cat Club, where the Maine Coon was the featured attraction. The CMCC was initiated by Alta Smith and Ruby Dyer of Skowhegan in 1953, and for ten years the group held shows at which the Maine Coon was the hometown hero. A godmother of the Maine Coon was Evelyn Whittemore. Her advocacy for the resurgence of the breed and the continuance of small regional shows led to one of her cats, Tiger Boy,

Solid Tiger Maine Coon neuter owned and bred by Mrs. Robert Whittemore.
1958 MAINE STATE CH. TIGER BOY (NEUTER).

Above: Circa 1920, this passel of feline beauties is ready for the cat show. Right: Judging at a turn-of-the-century cat show.

These Maine girls love their Maine cats.

claiming the 1958 Maine State Championship. Organizations like the CMCC and Maine Coon fanciers like Whittemore were responsible for putting the Maine Coon cat back on the map.

In the 1960s, a number of devoted Maine Coon breeders banded together and attempted to write an official, universally accepted breed standard. According to Beth Kus, "the core group of early enthusiasts were staunch in their efforts with their Maine cats, and with much work, an acceptable standard was developed comprising a composite of the best early cats."

In 1968, in Salisbury, Connecticut, the Maine Coon Breeders and Fanciers Association was formed, an organization still going strong today. Hornidge calls this development "the single strongest force in the last stage of the Maine Coon's comeback." The association's first big project was called a "show-in," with the goal to put as many Maine Coons in cat shows as they could. The group created a unified standard, and five years later all but one of the registering associations of North America had accepted the Maine Coon. Articles about the Maine Coon began appearing all over the world and that photogenic, handsome cat once again stole the hearts of the show halls, the breeding rings, and cat lovers.

Dirigo Maine-Origin Coons: Keeping the 'Maine' in Coon Cats

Beth Kus of Dirigo Maine Coon Cats has been breeding them for thirty-eight years and could be considered an incendiary of fierce devotion to the Maine component of the breed. She is a dyed-in-the-wool Mainer and although her husband's career brought them elsewhere during her breeding tenure, she came back to Maine to get cats that she believed to be the "genuine article." When she began showing her cats, she had an "aha" moment, realizing how few Maine-origin cats were actually in the show registers. This insight energized her to put the Maine origin back in and keep it going through the development of her own bloodline. She created the Dirigo bloodline using foundation cats as opposed to riding on anyone else's coat tails. She notes that this decision opened her up to a lot of flack from the cat community. But Beth carried on. She writes of the experience of getting her foundation cats: "With a strong sense of purpose and a deep love for the breed, my husband Crawford and I went back to Maine for our cats. Like the breeders who have gone to Turkey for their Turkish Angoras and Vans, to Thailand for their Korats, or to the Isle of Man for Manx, we went to the source of origin, home to Maine." But the search was not easy. "We naively thought they would be easy to find, but after searching

and visiting every farm in a thirty-mile stretch, only ordinary shorthairs were to be seen. We realized how rare natural Maine Coons really are." Through their tireless search, the Kuses were led to a Maine guide who raised Coon cats "because they were so nice to have around." They had found the perfect foundation kitten for their bloodline and the Dirigo family tree began in earnest.

At the height of her breeding career, Beth had a houseful of children. Her "hobby" kept her mind active as she contemplated pedigree and lineage while picking up Lego's or washing the dishes. Meanwhile, she devoured every bit of knowledge about breeder ethics, bloodlines, and genetics. And she bred gorgeous Maine Coons that were winning shows — she had no fewer than forty champions. "Every so often you get a star," she humbly says about her champions. Clearly, her cats are all stars, as they have been placed in homes all over the world, as far-flung as Cape Town, South Africa, and Moscow, Russia.

But Beth's biggest quest was traveling through the clouded gene pool of the Maine Coon to uncover a weak heart that had slipped into the breed. The show world, according to Kus, "was busy chasing rosettes but the cats they were showing weren't living past the age of three due to a serious heart condition." Beth Kus and a few other devoted breeders worked on figuring out what had created this genetic failure. The issue was resolved when a breeder came forward after determining it was her line and the mishap was fixed. But this genetic detective work made Beth even more committed to keeping the Maine-origin breed alive. Because, as she says, "Maine-origin cats had to be strong, had to adapt to the weather, had to be smart, and if they weren't healthy they didn't survive."

Now with the Dirigo line firmly in place and her daughter carrying on her own branch, Beth Kus is poised to retire. After years of having cats underfoot, she is still committed to the breed she calls "God's breed." She wouldn't choose any other cat because to her the Maine Coon is "everything good a cat is, trustworthy, intelligent, and sweet," and, thanks to her steadfast devotion, originating from Maine.

Tail
Long, equal to body in length (distance from end of rump to shoulders), wide at base and tapering. Fur full, long, and flowing.

Maine Coon Cat
BREED STANDARD

The Maine Coon is a solid, rugged cat and is America's oldest natural longhaired breed. Females are somewhat smaller than males, and allowance should be made for the slow maturation of the breed.

Coat Colors

All recognized colors. White trim around the chin and lip permitted except in solid-color cats. The following colors are among those recognized by most registering associations:

White, black, blue, red, cream.

Silver (chinchilla & shaded), blue-silver (chinchilla & shaded), cameo (shell, shaded, & smoke), cream cameo (shell, shaded, & smoke), black smoke, blue smoke, shaded tortoiseshell, shaded blue tortie, shaded torbie, shaded blue torbie.

Silver tabby (all patterns), blue-silver tabby (all patterns), cameo tabby (all patterns), cream cameo tabby (all patterns).

Shaded brown or golden tabby (all patterns), red tabby (all patterns), cream tabby (all patterns), brown tabby (all patterns), blue tabby (all patterns).

Bi-colors (solids with white), Parti-colors - tortoiseshell, torbie (patched tabby), calico, blue cream, tabby with white and other colors with white.

Disqualifications

Buttons, lockets, spots, overall even coat, short cobby body, crossed eyes, kinked tail, incorrect number of toes.

Penalties

Delicate bone structures, untufted paws, poor condition, nose break or bump, undershot chin, short rounded muzzle.

Coat

Fur on shoulders is short, gradually increasing in length along back and sides, ending in full britches and long, shaggy belly fur. Fur is soft but has body, falls smoothly, and lies close to the body. A slight undercoat is carried. A full ruff is not expected; however, there should be a frontal ruff beginning at the base of the ears.

Head

Medium in length and width, with a squareness to the muzzle. Allowance should be made for broadening in males. Cheek bones high. Nose medium in length with a gentle, concave curve and no break or bump. Chin firm and in line with upper lip and nose.

Ears

Large, wide at base, moderately pointed and well tufted. Set high on head approximately an ear's width apart. Lynx-like tipping is desirable.

Eyes

Large, wide set, slightly oblique setting. Eye color can be shades of green, gold, or copper, though white cats may be blue or odd-eyed. There is no relationship between eye color and coat color. Clarity of eye color is desirable.

Legs and Paws

Legs substantial, wide set, medium in length, contributing to a rectangular appearance. Paws large, round, well-tufted (five toes in front, four toes in back).

Cooper Ridge Cattery — Breeding with Integrity

High on a private ridge, nestled deep in the woods, sits an unassuming log home that has housed more than three hundred cats. And according to breeder Wanda Cooper, every cat born at the Cooper Ridge Cattery was bred with love and integrity. Wanda is now retired from the business, but the world of Maine Coons is still dear to her heart. Her lovely retired studs and queens follow her from room to room as she recounts the stories from her breeding years. When she first started out, she asked herself what she wanted to do with her cattery. The answer came loud and clear, breed with integrity. The thought of large-scale catteries turned her stomach and she knew she had no interest in locking up her cats for years. No, her cats would be raised underfoot and socialized. According to Wanda, "there is no way that a large commercial cattery can give cats any attention and the result is that you get a cat with an attachment disorder similar to when an orphan doesn't get held. The breeder can help determine a cat's personality." And for Wanda Cooper, her goal was to bring out the unique personality in every cat. Wanda named every single kitten, all two hundred and ninety of them. Each litter was given a letter and she would cycle through the alphabet, consulting baby name books. But aside from coming up with good names, her main goal as she sought to carry on the legacy of the majestic Coon, was the health of her cats. She says, "For me it was never about money. It was the cat's health above all." And out of all of those hundreds of kittens, she has had only two that had minor heart issues that were treated with medication. She continues, "To breed with integrity a breeder must select the kitten that is the strongest, healthiest, smartest, most playful, friendliest, and prettiest kitten in the litter. When you breed with these qualities in mind you can have a clear conscience that you are selling your customers an animal that will give them many years of contentment. It must also have most of the physical characteristics of the Maine Coon breed, such as a very distinctive classic or mackerel pattern of striping, lynx tips on the ears, the right-shaped muzzle, a nice ruff of fur on the neck, and a long plumy tail."

Cooper Ridge Coons live in fourteen states, mostly Massachusetts, but they have found homes in Iowa, Florida, Louisiana, and others as well. What Wanda loved about having a cattery was meeting so many different people and connecting through a cat. "It's not like selling a couch or a car because they don't return your love. I get emails and photos and stories all the time and it is very rewarding." Half of the people who Wanda sold cats to were retired and she knew that she was selling them something that they would nurture for the next fifteen or more years. There is only one thing that Wanda wishes as she puts her breeding days behind her, and that is to see every kitten she sold as a grown cat.

RESCUE CATS

Pussy's Port of Call

Pussy's Port of Call is a cattery and retreat for the pampered cat. Kitty condos overlook one of the most prized views in midcoast Maine, the rugged Penobscot Bay beneath the glorious Camden Hills. But this upscale waterfront cattery is also home to a very fortunate group of rescue cats. More than fifty-one cats have been found, left, or gifted to owners Richard and Peggy Wilson. Since there is no shelter in Waldo County, they have filled in and have hundreds of stories to share because of their efforts. They are the embodiment of Hemingway's quote, "one cat just leads to another."

Nicky is one of those lucky cats and he happens to be a Maine Coon. He began as a boarder when he was just a kitten and relished his time at Pussy's. Over the years, Richard and Peggy formed a deep bond with him and coaxed him through some of his kitty issues, such as being afraid of his shadow. When his owner fell ill, knowing how much Nicky loved Richard and Peggy, she asked if they would agree to take care of him after she passed. Soon after, Richard received a call and feared that Nicky's owner had died. Richard was reassured, however, that she had not in fact perished, but her clever, loyal Coon cat Nicky, knowing how much she hated the IVs and morphine drips, was ripping them out of her and, unfortunately, getting the morphine himself. So, that afternoon, Nicky found his port and became an office cat at Pussy's, where he has reigned supreme for more than ten years. Richard states that Nicky is perfect in his role of office cat because of the Maine Coon cat's exceedingly supervisory personality. They want to be involved in everything and be right in the midst of it all, especially the paperwork. But Nicky adds another quirky trait to his office duties — he will polish the left shoe of visitors gently with his paw. Not the right, only the left, and not everyone, only the lucky.

Throughout their years as cat lovers, the Wilsons have boarded, rescued, and owned several Maine Coon cats. They love all cats but agree there is something special about the Maine Coon. Peggy noted that a unique attribute about the breed is the length of time they take to develop not only physically but emotionally. "They ripen like a fine wine or cheese. But once they choose their people, the loyalty is unmatched."

One of their favorite cats of all time was a rescue Coon cat named Rocky. He was red with green eyes and had little flames of gold on the tips of his ears. He was a "hugger." He would take one paw, then the other, and place them on each shoulder, leaning in to give a full hug. For almost twelve years, Peggy and Richard were hugged daily by this great Coon cat, Rocky.

One Maine Coon who boarded with them for a long time, living to be almost twenty years old, was named Thistle. He was a bit prickly, hence the name, but he chose Peggy. All she would have to say is, "Thistle, would you like some tummy time," and the big guy would roll over on his back and drool while she rubbed his belly. His breath would slow, his eyes would close, and Peggy would inch away. Immediately he'd wake up, take his big furry paw and grab her hand, putting it right back on his belly.

Richard and Peggy insist that there is "no such thing as a bad cat, only a scared cat." And when a cat arrives with these exceedingly kind people, Peggy and Richard are willing to wait, sometimes for years, until a cat can trust them. They shared a story about a friend, a rather burly lobsterman with a big Maine Coon named Taylor. When Taylor was a kitten, he was brought to Pussy's in a lobster trap. Taylor was clearly miffed by this mode of transportation and his owner grumbled that all the cat did was hide. Richard advised that it sometimes takes a while for a cat to get used to things and to be patient. Nowadays, Taylor is amazingly people oriented.

The biggest Coon cat they ever boarded was named Archie. He had great big tufts on his ears and a monstrous tail and was as playful and loyal as can be, but still retained a wild look to him. They taught him the word "gentle" because at four months he had no idea of his impact and he was so huge already! One day, they were giving a tour to a local kindergarten, and Archie was draped over the cat furniture with all his appendages hanging off, and his tail slowly wagging from side to side. Richard and Peggy didn't even need to say, "use caution with Archie," as he just fixed those kids with a cold yellow stare, as if saying, "I eat little children," and those kids gave that giant a wide berth. Archie was the only cat that Richard and Peggy ever knew to howl at the full moon. But howl he did, while also playing tricks with a distinct sense of humor.

A quirky trait that Richard and Peggy have found with Maine Coons is that the larger the cat, the smaller the voice. An example of this is a huge Coon named Sullivan, who sings to himself, almost muttering under his breath. And then there is the relatively tiny Coon cat named Millie, a calico polydactyl, who has an amazingly sexy Lauren Bacall roar.

But after all the years, and all the Maine Coon stories, Peggy sums it up perfectly, "the feline idea of the rightness of things is especially true with a Maine Coon cat."

Franklin and Ozzie and the Cat Whisperer

Sky Taylor is an intuitive and Reiki practitioner who can now add pet psychic to her list of professions. She recently rescued a nine-year-old Maine Coon named Frank from the Old Town Animal Orphanage. For quite a while, prior to his adoption, Sky kept getting the name Frank whenever she did a reading. Lo and behold, when she began searching for a Maine Coon, a picture of a cat named Frank who was ready for adoption appeared on Facebook.

When Sky first met Frank she was a little hesitant because of his very big size — nineteen pounds — and he wasn't that sociable at the orphanage. But she had an intuition that he belonged with her and once she took him home, any sense of antisocial behavior completely disappeared and Frank became Franklin. Franklin was an injured stray, but according to Sky, you would never know. As she says about him, "He is so in tune with people and even though he is nine, he is as playful as a kitten."

But Franklin is not Sky's first Maine Coon. Ozzie was a retired Maine Coon stud who was given to Sky and her family. He adored being outside and Sky didn't have the heart to keep him in, but, sadly, Ozzie disappeared. After several months of tireless searching without any sign, a strange thing started happening

to Sky. At night when she was sleeping, she would wake to feel a weight on her feet. At first she thought it might be the way she had shifted the covers, but the episode repeated itself several more times. These visits were followed by a vivid dream in which Sky opened a window and Ozzy was sitting there looking at her. In dream terminology, when you open a window, a curtain, or a door, it is a sign you are ready to move on and are opening to a new chapter. Sky felt this was Ozzie's way of giving her permission to let him go, opening the way for Franklin's entrance.

So, as sad as it is not to have Ozzie in her life, Franklin has made himself very much at home. He even lets Sky perform Reiki on him, closing his eyes and tilting up his head as she lays her hands over him. Sky believes that "she just has a connection with Maine Coons. Smart isn't even the word for them." And for someone so attuned to the energies of people and animals, that is high praise.

Maine Coon Strays

Theresa Gargan, the manager of the Pope Memorial Humane Society of Knox County, Maine, is no stranger to cats, but out of the thousands that enter the shelter's doors, purebred Maine Coons are few and far between. Occasionally, a Maine Coon owner will fall on hard times and have to surrender their cat. "They don't sit around here long," Gargan notes. Purebred Maine Coons and Coon mixes leave the shelter quickly, as many people specifically request the breed on adoption applications. A common first question when someone walks through the door is whether there are any Coon cats. And looking around at the various long-haired cats around the lobby and cat rooms, Theresa shrugs and says, "There might be. So many cats are so mixed up at this point even some of those with shorter or medium length coats could have Maine coon in their bloodlines." But she knows the difference between "a really cool domestic long-hair with ear tufts" and a true blue Maine Coon cat.

When determining if a new arrival has a bit of the ol' Yankee cat, Gargan pays attention to the attitude — Maine Coons are dog-like and don't care about being around other cats. This is pretty noticeable when a cat is surrounded by twenty or thirty other felines. She can also tell by the structure of their faces, which have a bit more fullness to them and even have what she calls a "little chin."

The Humane Society of Knox County participates in a Trap, Neuter, Return program in conjunction with the Community Spay-Neuter Clinic out of Freeport, Maine. This successful program is funded by a grant from PetSmart Charities. The HSKC is responsible for trapping free-roaming cats in a wide geographic area. Many of these wild cats could carry the same "Maine" gene that is in Maine Coon cats. For, as breeder Beth Kus said, certain indigenous communities do still exist in Maine, New Hampshire, and the Maritime Provinces. One free-roaming cat named Rocky was trapped and neutered through this program. When the staff first found him he was a complete mess, but Gargan is convinced that he carried some strong Maine Coon genes. "He had that real sturdy frame and well-structured face, and

you could tell that he had really good bones." In fact, she said that if she were a breeder, she might have added him to her line to keep it healthy and authentic.

Just outside the cat enclosure sits a cat that the Humane Society employees have named Scar because he was so beaten up from his free-wheeling life. He is fascinated by the cats behind the fence, loves his daily meals, and is even visited each afternoon by his free-roaming lady friend (both are fixed), but even after six years, he still won't let anyone near him. One look at this regal cat with his torbie tones and large, well-boned structure and you cannot help thinking of the long line of ancestors going back to the origins of the breed in this same coastal area hundreds of years ago. Scar and Rocky are two examples of the same kind of "survival of the fittest" evolution that formed this long-lasting and iconic breed.

How to Tell if Your Rescue Cat is a Maine Coon

"I found this beautiful tabby with long hair and a big "M" on its forehead." "I live in Indiana and have a cat with big fluffy tufts coming out of its ears." "My cat has huge paws and a big, bushy tail." "Is my cat a Maine Coon?" The traits mentioned above all apply to the Maine Coon cat, but determining the whole of the cat, according to breeder Beth Kus, depends on some very specific qualities. For many of us have found a cherished long-haired mix and looked on the Internet hoping to confirm that it really is a Maine Coon. But be forewarned, says Beth, for "you may feed a look-alike cat lobster all of its life and bless it with a map of Maine, but that will not make it a true Maine Coon."

So how can you tell if your beloved foundling is of the regal Maine Coon class? Location, location, location. If you happen to live in Maine, or on the New England seaside, or even in the Canadian Maritimes, then there is at least a chance that you have stumbled upon a naturally bred non-pedigreed Maine Coon. But they are not plentiful even there, although small indigenous populations do exist.

The colors and markings of a Maine Coon are universal among cat colorations. The only combination that the Maine Coon color wheel doesn't contain are the pointed versions of the Siamese and Himalayan. The other mark that people often assume is exclusive of the Maine Coon is the famed M on the cat's

Maine Coon Cat

Norwegian Forest Cat

Siberian Cat

forehead. This, however, is a typical marking on tabbies in general and does not necessarily indicate your cat is a Maine Coon. There are many types of long-haired mixed breeds, so looking at the specific quality of a cat's coat is another step in uncovering the Maine Coon mystery. Maine Coons have a very specific shagginess about them. Again, according to Beth Kus, "a cat showing Maine Coon heritage will have a long, shaggy, uneven coat that is short over the shoulders and longer toward the tail. It is made up of guard hairs that are glossy and somewhat coarse, and these are longer than the insulating hairs. The insulating hairs will be satiny-soft." It is not unusual for many long-haired varieties to have a ruff, fur between the toes, and a fluffy tail.

The body of a Maine Coon is also different than its long-haired kin. The Maine Coon has a stretched-out rectangular shape as opposed to the more square body of Persians or Angora mixes. The head of a Maine Coon varies from a more typical domestic long-hair as it is more angular with ears that are significantly pointed. Beth Kus explains the fineries of the Maine Coon's distinguished facial shape: "The head of a Maine Coon is recognized by its series of intersecting angles, the ears are set at angles to the nose, the muzzle is squared off, and elongated very slightly, and the profile has a flow like a gentle ski jump."

Okay, so we have checked off location, coat, color, forehead M, body, head shape, but what about the remarkable personality of the Maine Coon. Some of the quirky traits of these cats are unique to the breed, so pay attention if your cat loves water, acts like a dog, plays fetch, and is exceptionally teachable.

Here is how Beth Kus breaks it down: "If a cat meets all of the descriptions above and is from Maine, or the Maritime Provinces, or the seacoast area of New Hampshire, it is a Maine Coon. If a cat meets the descriptions but is from other parts of the USA or Canada, it is a part-Maine Coon. If a cat meets most of the description above, it is a domestic long-hair with some Maine Coon in it. No matter how much or how little, a Maine Coon cat will bless its owners in a way that no other cat can."

So, is your cat a Maine Coon cat?

Caring for and Grooming a Maine Coon

Having evolved naturally by survival of the fittest; the Maine Coon is a breed that is fairly low maintenance. Here are some tips to keep your biggest domestic cat looking its best:

✓ Maine Coon coats are water resistant, allowing the cat to float and swim easily. They don't mind water and some will let you give them an occasional bath or shower.

✓ The long coat is easy to care for and rarely tangles. A good combing once or twice a week will keep the coat in good condition. Combing can also help you detect potential health problems early.

✓ Trim their claws regularly. The more often you trim their claws as a kitten, the easier it will be when they are older.

✓ Check their teeth regularly. If anything seems out of the ordinary, consult your veterinarian.

✓ Maine Coons often play in their drinking water. Make sure fresh, clean water is available at all times.

living with a
maine coon cat:
OWNERS' STORIES

Three Cats Under Four

Ironically, Kimmy Lockie started her love affair with Maine Coons in a country about as far away from Maine as you can get — New Zealand. Kimmy had recently married a Kiwi and they decided to move back to Duncan's home turf. Although she loved it there, Kimmy was a bit lonely without her family nearby and so the idea of a cat occurred to her as a way to remedy this bout of homesickness. The couple heard about a kennel that was searching for a home for a Maine Coon and although they met the cat and fell in love, it didn't end up working out. But that first encounter with a Maine Coon ignited something in Kimmy and she knew from that moment on that it was her breed. Her mom was living in Maine and so the thought of having a connection to the state from so far away was appealing. Searching the islands over, Kimmy and Duncan turned up an amazing-looking silver-and-black-smoke Maine Coon that they named Wolfie Boy.

Kimmy and Duncan decided to spend a summer in Maine, leaving Wolfie Boy in the care of some dear friends, but after the summer in Camden, they realized they wanted to stay. Again the Hemingway quote, "one cat just leads to another," proved its accuracy and they were tempted by another Maine Coon. Welcome Cheeto, a gorgeous red male given to Kimmy by Duncan as a birthday present. Two days later, Kimmy went back to Cold River Cattery in Augusta to get yet another Maine Coon, this time a tabby female named Babycakes as an anniversary present for Duncan. Duncan, this former non-cat person, was smitten. He says, "Before Cheeto I wasn't a cat person at all. I just thought cats did their own thing and didn't pay any attention to people. Cheeto completely changed my mind. He was super-good looking and

affectionate." Bringing Wolfie Boy back to Maine proved too big a challenge and the family taking care of him was so in love they didn't want to let him go. Kimmy and Duncan still get regular Wolfie Boy updates and he is very much part of their lives serving as their "satellite cat."

So with three Maine Coons under their belt, Kimmy thought it might be fun to have the experience of kittens. This idea prompted Phil, another fiery red, to join the clan and attempt to mate with Babycakes. Unfortunately, Babycakes had uterine complications and wasn't able to carry a litter. But Phil makes up for any lack of kittens, as he is packed with personality. Each day he wakes Kimmy and Duncan by dropping one of his sponge balls for an immediate game of wake up and fetch. Sometimes to try to gain a few more minutes of sleep, Duncan hides the balls in the drawer of the night table, but Phil knows how to open the drawer and gets them anyway. Phil uses his huge snowshoe paws for many feats but especially loves to steal potato chips out of the bag. Phil likes to perch on the television stand but is only drawn to this spot for his favorites, golf, the Nature Channel, and surfing — everything else is not worth the leap.

While Phil is the most theatrical of the bunch, the Maine Coon comes out in all of them when Kimmy takes a bath. All three line up on the rim of the tub while Phil dips his entire leg in the water, providing a whirlpool effect for his dear mom. All of this pampering of their mom is sure to get them one of their famous cat-nip parties where they can pull out all their kitten-like moves, proving they are incredible examples of the breed.

Moomoo Comes Home

The feline version of *Lassie Comes Home* has yet to be written, but the following story of a Maine Coon and his adventure has much of the same heartfelt emotion. Moomoo was always just the best cat, according to his owner, Sasha. He never did anything wrong, never hissed or scratched, even when the youngest of the family dragged him around or sat on his tail. As befits a majestic Maine Coon, his temperament was gentle and even-keeled and he had the patience of a saint.

But this gentle guy disappeared three years ago. Moomoo's family looked everywhere, at every pound and neighbor's house until they began to assume the worst. After three and a half months without Moomoo, the phone rang. The Rockland Animal Shelter had found him, identifying him by his implanted microchip. Apparently he had gained entry into an elderly couple's home and immediately went up to them and sat on their laps. Despite his scraggly and dirty appearance, they knew he was too nice to be a stray. When the family got the news, they all loaded into the car, even Sasha's mother who was visiting from Russia, to bring Moomoo home. He had lost a third of his weight and they found a BB pellet lodged in his side. He looked like a battle-weary veteran carrying the weight of the world. As they loaded Moomoo in the car, his lifelong motion sickness reignited and he threw up all over them. They didn't care, they had Moomoo back safe and sound.

An employee at the shelter told the family that people often steal Maine Coon cats because they are valuable and have a certain cachet. There is also a chance that he got into a workman's car and was thrown out of it at some point after he most likely got sick. Sasha just wishes he could talk, "He has this amazing survival story," she says.

But as Moomoo returned to his rightful place with his family, he was just as sweet as ever. He still snores and drools, but he also cuddles with everyone, especially when they are sick. He wags his tail when he sees any of his family and especially as he waits for what Sasha calls his "kitty pâté."

Moomoo has a distant cousin connecting him to the origin stories of the Maine Coon. Sasha hails from Russia and remembers having a cat that looked just like Moomoo when she was little, named Murzik. Murzik was a Siberian cat that the family acquired during the few years they lived in Siberia. According to Sasha, the two cats are dead-ringers for each other, both in looks and personality, and share an extreme intelligence. But Murzik had one up on Moomoo, as he taught himself to pee in Sasha's brother's training potty. Interestingly enough, according to some Maine Coon origin theories, Siberian cats are direct ancestors of Maine Coons. Jane Martinke writes, "We could easily decide that their forebears were the now unknown Russian longhairs which once flourished on the continent and the British Isles since those were tabbies." As Sasha looked at images of Siberian cats, she exclaimed, "That is Moomoo, exactly." Who knows, Moomoo and Murzik, two cats from two different countries sharing a singular gene pool? As Moomoo continues to put his long journey of survival behind him, maybe one more journey to his mother's homeland awaits him.

So, You Think
You Have a Show Cat?

Maine Coon cats are indeed show stopping and gorgeous in their own right — some even meet the high expectations that make them a hit in the show halls. Embarking on the life of a show-cat owner is not for the faint of heart. Cats that are shy, nervous, or suffer from motion sickness will not do well with this kind of lifestyle. Keep in mind, too, that the show circuit is not an inexpensive path with the various show fees, travel accessories, and even airfare. But some cats were born for a life in the show ring, so why deny them the opportunity to experience it and give the world the benefit of your cat's regal beauty. Following are some tips for curious cat owners who might be toying with the pursuit of this hobby.

Attend a cat show as a spectator to get a feel for the ambiance and the wide variety of cats on display. Walk around to get a sense of the layout, the people who are involved, and even the vendors. Talk to as many people as you can and learn what it takes to get involved in this endeavor. Shows are listed in most major cat publications and Web sites and are usually organized by region.

Study the show standards for the Maine Coon detailing what judges look for in competitions. Unless you plan to enter your cat under the household pet category, the breed standards are important. While you are at it, order a copy of the Cat Fanciers Association Show Rules. These rules give vital information about the responsibilities for exhibitors as well as entry procedures and eligibility.

When you decide on which show to enter and in which category, contact the entry clerk for that particular show and request an entry form. Some shows have limited entries and some do not offer the HHP category (household pet category). Once you have filled out your paperwork, make sure to send it back to the entry clerk for processing at least two months before the show.

Once your cat is accepted, it is time for the salon. Give that famous Maine Coon coat some extra fluffing and a "show bath" and your beauty will be ready for the pageant. Serious beauty products exist to degrease, fluff, eliminate static, and condition your cat's coat. Many people use specific coloring shampoos to bring out the highlights of their cat's coat — for example, Nexus Simply Silver for a white or silver cat. For a very thorough discussion on the particularities of the "show bath," go to the website of Cascade Mountain Maine Coons at www.cascademountain.net.

Turn your cat carrier into a show-mobile by hanging "show curtains." These essential curtains prevent your cat from the distraction of neighboring cats and keep cat fights to a minimum. Some show enthusiasts go wild with this decorative element, matching fabrics to accentuate the best qualities of their cat. After creating the curtains, outfit your cat's carrier with some of their comfort items and a few of their favorite toys to occupy them on the road. Make sure to pack food, dinnerware, and a litter pan, as well as grooming supplies for a quick brush prior to your kitty's debut.

Perhaps your cat is not a natural beauty but has more of an athletic bent? Well, luck is on your side, as cat agility is a growing feline phenomenon. These competitions are modeled after dog agility contests and allow cats to try their paw at a varying level of obstacles. Some cats speed through the obstacles like Olympians, while others have to be praised, prodded, and occasionally removed from the course. Vicki Shields, one of the pioneers of this movement, declares that "this whole thing about cats being untrainable is ingrained in society and it's a myth." Anyone who owns a Maine Coon will rally behind Shields. Many of the cat agility adoptees use various forms of cajoling or training, such as clicker training and reward-based incentives, similar to dog training. But the difference is, as Shields testifies, "cats are

very smart and very trainable, but they're not dogs. They don't take orders. They will do things you want them to do for praise and for fun — and if they want to do it." The wanting to do it is the key, for even certified agility contest ringmasters concur that sometimes a cat that took an amazing run one time will simply sit in the middle of the course on the next round and give themselves a bath. "Indeed, part of the appeal is the possible train-wreck aspect that proves cats are independent thinkers," says Sharon Peters, who reported on this new avenue of cat competitions for *USA Today*. But if you think your Maine Coon is trainable, likes a challenge, and has some graceful moves, then why not give cat agility a try at your next cat show. Many cat shows currently have this option and most offer "practice runs" for first-timers. Plus, any cat can be entered, even a Maine Coon mix, opening up the show hall to a broader spectrum of felines and creating a new category of "cathletes."

coon cats that made a mark
ON LITERATURE

Togus — A Coon Cat Finds a Home and Fame

❝ He found us by chance, totally by chance. A huge, somewhat scroungy Maine Coon cat, rescued with more than two dozen others from a place that could no longer care for them. Now, a decade later, it almost seems we were predestined to have Togus the cat be part of our lives. **❞**

—Don Carrigan

There is the story of Togus, from the book *Togus, A Coon Cat Comes Home,* written by Don Carrigan and illustrated by Thomas Block, and then there are the hundreds of other Togus stories that, as one woman from the Maine State House remarked, "just make you feel good." Togus was one of those exceptional cats, "part-human," his mother Donna always said, that truly make a mark on the world. With his giant paw print and all twenty-six pounds and thirty-six inches of length, Togus made an impact that even his passing in 2012 does nothing to diminish.

Don and Donna Carrigan didn't expect a Togus in their lives, what they were expecting was a Maine Coon kitten. And that call came one morning from Judy Doe at the Louis Doe Home Center in Newcastle,

Maine. She told them that twenty-nine Maine Coon cats and kittens had just arrived and all of them needed homes. When the Carrigans walked into Louis Does, the store was transformed into a cat-cage jungle. Cages were piled all over and stacked up to the ceiling. Judy pulled out a beautiful six-month-old tiger at the same moment that Don spotted Togus. Don yelled to Donna, "You've got to see this fella over here." Togus had been badly matted so two-thirds of his body was shaved, he had pointy ears and a bobcat look about him. As Don was taking him out of his cage, Donna was saying, "No, no, no, we already have two cats at home and we came for a kitten today." But as Togus kept coming and coming, Donna set aside her reluctance and nodded, knowing they just had to have him.

He came with the name Tango but when Don and Donna looked at his battle worn coat and thought about his recent travails, they thought he looked like a beat up old vet. A Togus. Donna's father had been at Togus Veteran's Hospital and so the name felt right.

Don recounts Togus's arrival home in his children's book and the transformational moment, two days later, when Togus finally emerged from the secluded crate in the laundry room, sauntered across the kitchen floor, stretching his long body to make himself look even bigger, and jumped onto Donna's lap. Donna didn't know what to do so she gripped the sides of the chair and waited for the twenty-six pound cat to either swipe her or settle in. They stared at each other in stunned silence. Then Togus reached his front legs up to snuggle, and in that moment Togus was home. For the next ten years, Donna's lap was his oasis. Every morning, once Donna had gotten her coffee and turned on the news, Togus would be right at her feet. She'd put her hands out and he'd jump up and sit in her lap. Maine Coons, especially really big ones, are not typically lap cats, but as it turned out, Togus was anything but typical.

Little did the Carrigans know that this cat was destined for great things. Just as they found him by chance at Louies Does, Togus found celebrity the same

way. For decades, Don Carrigan covered the storm team for WCSH Channel 6 and when he moved back to the midcoast, he continued this coverage out of Rockland. When the technical center went bad, the producer suggested that Don call in from home. Don's storm update calls were accompanied by a picture of Don in his kitchen with Togus resting on the kitchen table. Lee Nelson asked from the studio why Don's dog was on the table. Don replied, "That's not a dog, that's our twenty-six-pound Maine Coon cat, Togus." A legend was born. The next time storm coverage was on air, the announcer said, "And now let's head to Don and Togus." Before long, the audio clip was replaced by video and Togus appeared in living rooms all over the state of Maine. A year later,

John Blunda created a Facebook page for Togus. A brief mention of this on the morning news prompted the number of Togus fans to rise from 1,000 to 5,000. Today, Togus has more than eleven thousand fans. How do you explain a cat having such a huge fan base? Don Carrigan offers the following explanation.

"The winter the Facebook page began, I mentioned to a woman at the State House that the whole thing seemed crazy — all these people wanting to be online fans of a cat. "It isn't crazy at all," she said. "Look around. It's winter, the economy's terrible, people are having a hard time. He just makes you feel good." And maybe it is that simple. A big, fluffy, friendly cat with remarkable ears, a striking, lion-like face with enormous eyes, looking at you from his kitchen table. There was just something about that face and those eyes that made people (well, most people) want him at their own table. We got a few comments, of course, from grumpy folks disgusted that we'd let the cat on the table. But far more came from those who seemed to love Togus as much as we did. "He just makes you feel good."

The perch where Togus conducted his forecasts overlooks a big bay window onto the Carrigans' deck where a variety of bird feeders are strung along the perimeter. At night, a big insulated shade was lowered to save heat. When Togus arrived in the morning, the shade was lifted like the opening of a Broadway musical so Togus could then spend hours watching the aviary dance outside. The perch, sadly vacated by Togus, is now kept warm by Grady, the Carrigan's ninety-pound golden retriever. Now there really is a dog on the table.

But no one can fill Togus's shoes because there has never been a cat like him. He had this interesting presence — lionesque with those huge eyes that looked half human. And then there were those tucked-down ears. People often told Don that Togus was a Scottish Fold, not a Maine Coon. But Togus's ears weren't always folded. The look was the result of dual aneurisms that required double surgeries. Don says, "I think as it turned out, he didn't have those lynx-tip ears, but the way his ears ended up after his surgery gave him a very distinctive look, those flat ears and the way he fixed you with that deep stare. You couldn't take your eyes off him."

Don wrote that Togus was "in looks, temperament, and attitude, perfectly suited for stardom." And in his stardom he played a myriad of roles — he was the Grand Marshal for the Damarscotta Pumpkin Festival, he cut the ribbon for a new animal shelter, he rode the train to collect coats for kids, and he even sat on the governor's desk. Although the orders were changed, a Maine National Guard Unit heading to Afghanistan was set to bring a giant cutout of Togus with them to the war. But perhaps the most satisfying role of all was as star of his very own successful children's book. At the many events and readings surrounding the book launch, Togus sat regally in his large dog crate with the door open, letting hand after hand pet him, never once swiping or hissing. At one of the first events for the book in Norway, Maine, a woman shared that she had read the book to her thirty at-risk students. Every one of them wrote letters to Togus, writing things such as, "I hope I find love like Togus did."

"See, that was the main thing, Togus taught people to never give up hope," Don says. "So now he's gone, and there is a tremendous hole in our lives. We are heartbroken, of course, but also very grateful. We shared ten years with an incredible creature. "Member of the family" doesn't do him justice. He was a presence in our lives every day. He was part of who we are. Everywhere I go, people ask about Togus. "How's the cat? Where's the cat today?" Every day, every news assignment for the past six years or more, people have asked the question. Togus, the huge and friendly Maine Coon cat, was truly larger than life."

The Cat Made Me Buy It

Maine Coon cats not only made a distinctive mark on literature, but they also clawed their way to the top of the advertising world from the Victorian age throughout the mid-twentieth century. The long-haired beauties were often placed next to a rosy-cheeked child, as in the Kellogg's ad for Toasted Corn Flakes that admonishes the cereal is for "Kiddies not Kitties."

Cigars peaked in popularity during the Victorian age, as did Maine Coons, and the two were often paired. According to Alice L. Muncaster and Ellen Yanow, authors of *The Cat Made Me Buy It,* "Cigar boxes featuring cats undoubtedly appealed to Victorian women and children, and these boxes were likely to be treasured and kept around the home so that the pictures on the labels could be enjoyed again and again."

In 1900, Ivory Soap launched a stunning Art Nouveau print ad featuring a white coon cat surrounded by envious black cats. The tag line, "It Floats," might not only refer to Ivory Soap's ability to float but also to the uncanny characteristic of the Maine Coon's coat.

Another product that highlighted the Maine Coon during this same period was the popular Corticelli Silk Thread. The company espoused the thread's silky, lustrous qualities, which were well matched with the Maine Coon's luminous coat. Corticelli's advertisements, thanks to the allure of the stunning Maine Coons, won the company a gold medal for advertising in 1901.

Maine Coons continue to be the darling of the cat world with their sweet, charming faces and their long, gleaming coats epitomizing the coziness and warmth of a good old-fashion American cat.

"For Kiddies
Not
Kitties"

Kellogg's
TOASTED
CORN
FLAKES

W. K. Kellogg

IVORY SOAP 99 44/100 PER CENT PURE

ENVY

IT FLOATS

ONE DOZEN SPOOLS
WARRANTED 50 YARDS

Corticelli
SPOOL SILK
THE DRESSMAKER'S FAVORITE
CORTICELLI SILK MILLS
THE CORTICELLI SILK COMPANY ~ FLORENCE, MASS., U.S.A.

ANOTHER "HIT" BY THE WRITERS OF "WHAT D'YE MEAN YOU LOST YER DOG"
THE PUSSY CAT RAG
(KITTY, KITTY,
KITTY, KITTY)

WORDS BY
THOS. S. ALLEN
MUSIC BY
JOSEPH M. DALY
& THOS. S. ALLEN

Hodge — The Bookstore Cat

ABCD Books in Camden, Maine, was a renowned treasure trove of antiquarian books, known not only for its incredible selection and lovely shop space, but also for Hodge, the Maine Coon cat that called it home. His official name was Hodgie Burr, and he was a rescue cat brought to live at the store by the owners.

All who encountered him could attest that he was an extraordinary cat. He easily mastered standard tricks like catching a ball and coming when called, and, according to former store owner Barrie Pribyl, "He could have been a member of MENSA." His biggest accomplishment, though, was entertaining passersby from his storefront window perch. One of his most celebrated window antics happened during the Christmas holiday, when a crèche was displayed in the window. The crèche was filled with the usual layer of hay and Hodge loved the feel of the straw beneath him, so each day he climbed into the scene, taking his nap at the feet of baby Jesus.

Hodge tolerated everyone, from customers petting him to children who eagerly sought him out. He often followed customers around until they remarked about how glorious he was and how utterly handsome. Only after that proper recognition did he gracefully regain his post. Hodge never got into trouble or shredded anything, an important attribute for a bookstore cat. The only minor concern was that he sometimes got a little grumpy and hid out for a while. One time, the staff really could not locate Hodge, so Barrie sent a letter to the local paper saying that Hodge had gone for ice cream and would be back soon. The community went wild in their concern, asking continuously if Hodge had been found. Of course, he reemerged unscathed in his own time and from who knows where, and resumed his window bathing. So happy were people to see Hodge in the window that they often forgot their manners and tapped on the window to say hello to dear old Hodge. This began happening too much for his taste and so Barrie promptly posted a sign that read, "Do not tap on the window while Hodge is sleeping. How would you like to be abruptly woken from a nap?" And from that point on, he was able to fall into his deep slumbers undisturbed, his large, furry body pressed up against the glass. At one point, the YMCA childcare came for a visit to verify that Hodge was real and not a stuffed cat. The children were quite surprised when he opened his eyes, stretched into "cat pose," and seemed to say, "Here I am, ready to be petted and adored."

Hodge loved to get his picture taken and knew instinctively how to pose. So much so, that postcards were made of him and sold in the store, and an ABCD Books calendar was made with his regal presence gracing every page. Hodge received letters from all over, but the most memorable was a Christmas card informing him that he was in the Metropolitan Museum of Art. Apparently, an employee of the Met had brought one of the postcards of Hodge back to his post and displayed it prominently on his desk for all to see. Hodge was even included twice in a nationally distributed cat calendar.

ABCD Books closed its doors in 2009, and the most common questions that former owner Barrie Pribyl receives, even more than if she misses the store, is where is Hodge, how is he, and do you miss him. "He really connected with people," says Pribyl. But despite the years of adulation, Hodge seems to be enjoying his retirement from manning the bookstore window. He has found a new window to rest in at a former employee's house, away from the paparazzi.

Trout and My Cat, Coon Cat

There are many ways to celebrate a book contract, but when that book happens to be about a Maine Coon cat, what better way than getting a real live model. Jeannie Brett has illustrated many books throughout her career, but perhaps the most life changing was illustrating *My Cat, Coon Cat,* written by Sandy Fuller. Jeannie's daughter surprised her with a Maine Coon of her own and Jeannie's life and career will forever benefit from the gift. After extensive research, Jeannie's daughter found Trout at G.G. Legacy Breeders in Massachusetts and, according to Brett, he is "like no cat she has ever had."

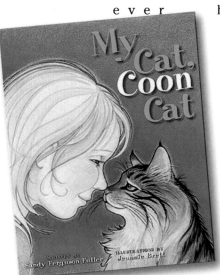

Jeannie describes Trout as "kind of dog-like," as he trots along beside her, enjoys nice walks on a leash, and loves a good game of fetch. He digs through his toy basket to find just the right toy and Jeannie and Trout even play hide and seek. After relating all of these stories, Jeannie laughs and admits that her family thinks she has gone a bit over the edge.

But the handsome tabby was a perfect model for the eight months Jeannie spent creating the exquisite illustrations for *My Cat, Coon Cat.* She says of the experience, "I tried to capture the spirit of a young cat, the way they are so bouncy and happy. So his poses were influential, especially the one where he keeps his tail up so high." Jeannie snapped hundreds of photos on her iPhone and Trout barely sat still for any of them. But as the book attests, she did manage to perfectly capture the activity, haughtiness, and amazing fluffiness of a Maine Coon.

The cat in *My Cat, Coon Cat* is shy and Trout can be shy as well, but definitely not around Jeannie. The two are constant companions as he frolics in Jeannie's studio. He may even go on an airplane for a fly-fishing trip to Wyoming to meet his namesakes. But whatever the adventure, this stunning Maine Coon is already the star of his own story and will continue to delight illustrator Jeannie Brett.

finding a
MAINE COON CAT

After reading all about this amazing breed, why spend another day without a gentle giant by your side. So where do you begin the search? At the pet shop around the corner? Absolutely not! No breeder worth their salt would ever sell to a pet shop. Buying a cat from this venue will leave you no way to determine how that kitten's first days were spent, what its pedigree looks like, or to see with your own eyes the conditions in which the kitten was raised. Another big no-no is purchasing a Maine Coon from what in the cat world is termed a backyard breeder. These breeders do so for the sake of making a profit and not with the goal of improving the breed or creating show-quality cats. They are out of touch with the rest of the breeding world and so have no one to help them if a problem comes up in one of their bloodlines. However, by asking the right questions you can avoid falling into the backyard breeder trap.

The absolute best way to find a Maine Coon kitten is by going to the place where breeders of high standards go, a cat show. Cat shows allow you to find a breeder who you trust and with whom you might want to establish a relationship as your kitten becomes available. Don't expect to walk away from a cat show with a kitten as they most likely will not be in attendance, and reputable breeders will probably have waiting lists and will want to know more about you and your home before they allow one of their cats to live with you. Those are the qualities you want to see in a reputable breeder.

If you cannot find a cat show in your area, you can peruse the advertisements in various magazines such as *Cat Fancy,* but many backyard breeders also advertise in these venues so you will need to do solid research. A nice referral option is the Web site of the esteemed Maine Coon Breeders and Fanciers Association. This Web site has a national listing of Maine Coon breeders and, although the organization

itself cannot recommend specific breeders, they will steer you as you begin your search. The fact that a breeder has registered with a national organization is a good sign and shows they are invested in their reputation.

Once you find a cattery that is nearby, visiting is advisable. Seeing the actual site where the kittens are born will allow you to evaluate the cleanliness of the facility, meet the adult cats, even the parents, and determine if you are comfortable developing a relationship with this particular breeder. Breeder Cat Moody, from Stormwatch Maine Coons, states that the most important question to answer when visiting a cattery is, "Do the breeding cats and resulting kittens seem like beloved family members?" If the cats are shy and aloof, even nervous, needing to be pulled out from a hiding spot to meet you, that is a dramatic red flag. These cats are a direct representation of how the breeder is handling their litters. Noting where the kittens are being raised is important. If they are housed in a part of the house with only the mother cat, this would sound an alarm for proper socialization. Also, if there are more than two or three litters at one time, it might be more of a kitten mill than a quality breeder who is going to devote a lot of time to their cats.

Some Questions You Should Always Ask a Breeder

The following list of questions was compiled by Cat Moody, who says, "You are making a big investment in both time and money. A vague answer or two might be expected, but most of these questions should be answered to your satisfaction — or go elsewhere.

Do you show your cats?
Is your cattery registered?
May I look at the cat's pedigree?
What are the health problems of this breed?
How old will the kitten be before it comes home?
Will the kitten be registered?
Will I get a contract and written health warranty?
What if I am interested in showing or breeding?
Do you give your own shots?

After hearing the answers from the breeders, it is time to listen to your gut. If you have any sense of hesitation, move along. Does the breeder seem friendly and anxious to answer your questions? If they seem annoyed with you, move on. There are many cats to choose from and many other catteries out there to work with. If you are okay with the answers, then it might be the breeder's turn to inquisition you. Again, Cat Moody advises, "Don't be surprised if some of the questions seem personal — these kittens are not commodities to the reputable breeder. They are little lives that we have planned, assisted in their births, raised with love, and probably have slept on our heads for the last three months. Most of us are proud of what we do, and happy to hear from informed pet buyers — it makes us feel more confident in the commitment the pet buyer intends to make to this kitten."

There are many personalities and styles of Maine Coons to choose from, ranging from the feral to the sweet. Knowing what you are looking for, whether it is a boy or a girl or a certain color is up to you, but often a kitten will "pick" you. A good breeder is helpful in choosing a kitten with a temperament that suits particular situations. For example, if you have other cats, a dog, or young children, temperament selection will be vital in ensuring a good match.

Sara Holding a Cat — vaguely resembling a Maine Coon — 1908 painting by Mary Cassatt.

And last but not least, there is the issue of how much you can expect to pay for these pedigreed, well-socialized, beautiful Maine Coons. Yes, they are a bit pricey — in the range of $400 to $1,000 for "pet quality" kittens. Show-quality kittens are vastly more expensive and breeders often have long waiting lists for those desirable kittens. Chances are the average cat owner would not even notice the difference between a "pet quality" and a "show quality" kitten. It might be as simple as a slight angle in the eyes or a white spot on the chest that does not work for that breeder. Cat Moody offers this word of caution, "Beware of breeders who say that every kitten they produce is a 'Top Show Quality' kitten." For the responsible breeder, the cost of this cat barely meets the cost of breeding, showing, and caring for the cattery. Buying a Maine Coon is an investment, but one that will give a lifetime of returns.

So remember to find a good cattery, ask lots of questions, and take your time. Every single kitten is adorable. When looking at that tiny ball of fluff, it is nearly impossible to make a rational decision. But try your best, because if you pay attention to your head as well as your heart, the right Maine Coon will come your way and change your life forever.

The Maine Coon Cat Nation Web site has a comprehensive state-by-state list of breeders to help you find a cattery: maine-coon-cat-nation.com/maine-coon-cat-breeders-usa.html.

No cat can be truly perfect and although the Maine Coon comes very close, there are a few genetic diseases to be aware of as you search for a kitten. A good breeder will work scrupulously to eliminate health issues from their bloodlines, but before making a purchase, be sure to ask the breeder if any of their cats have suffered from any of the following diseases that have been identified in Maine Coon cat lines. According to veterinarian Kate Bergen Pierce, DVM, "Responsible breeders will perform genetic testing on their breeding animals and should be open to any questions you may have about these diseases.

Hypertrophic cardiomyopathy is the most well known and devastating of the genetic diseases to which Maine Coons, among other cat breeds, are prone. It causes a thickening of the heart wall, making the organ less elastic and the chambers smaller, thus reducing the heart's ability to pump efficiently. The weakened blood flow often leads to clotting, which can result in sudden fatality. The difficulty with this disease is that it can be asymptomatic so that cat owners don't know their cat is sick until it suddenly dies. "It's such a shame," says veterinarian Pierce. "It is challenging to even detect a murmur or any other signs to let you know this disease is taking place in your cat's heart." Often this disease strikes when a cat is still quite young, between the ages of three and five, which makes the spontaneous death even more shocking.

You probably hear more about **hip dysplasia** in dogs than in cats, yet according to Professor Jerold Bell, DVM, of Tufts University, 22.6% of Maine Coon cats are affected by the disease. Knowing how to move more carefully or resist jumping, Maine Coons fare better than their canine counterparts with this hereditary defect that causes a malformed hip socket joint. But dysplasia can lead to arthritis and a life of coping with

a fair amount of pain. Since cats generally put on a stiff upper lip when dealing with pain, they might not even show a limp.

Spinal muscular atrophy is a tragic genetic disease that affects the nerves and muscles along the spine, causing them to lose their musculature so that the cat's entire back end becomes weakened and atrophied. This mutation becomes visible when a kitten is only three or four months old. According to the Web site PawPeds. com, "By five or six months they are too weak in the hindquarters to readily jump up on furniture and often have a clumsy landing when jumping down. The long-haired Maine Coon may hide it, but a careful feeling of the limbs will reveal reduced muscle mass." Despite how debilitating this disease sounds, kittens with this condition are not in any discomfort, are not incontinent, and can often live comfortably for many years.

Don't be too frightened. None of these diseases is exclusive to Maine Coon cats, particularly the heart defect, which can be common in large cats in general. The best tool of all is a good veterinarian who you can trust and who will help you to rule out any of these problems. Dr. Pierce encourages Maine Coon owners to have their cat's blood tested to determine if their cat has hypertrophic cardiomyopathy or to give their cat a specific genetic test for spinal muscular atrophy. "Although," she says, "not much can be done, at least you can prepare yourself if this is in your cat's genetic makeup." Veterinarians can use x-rays to screen for hip dysplasia and ultrasound to detect any thickening of the heart wall. Knowing that your cat is free of any of these diseases would be worth the cost of prescreening and give you the peace of mind of knowing your cat is guaranteed to live a long, healthy life.

RESOURCES

Maine Coon Rescue

304 First Avenue West
Franklin, KY 42134
mainecoonrescue.net

The Maine Coon Rescue is a nationwide non-profit organization dedicated to rescuing Maine Coons and Maine Coon mixed cats. They have a handy pet finder map to see if there are cats in your area. They have a foster program if you are interested in fostering a Maine Coon until they can find it a forever home.

Maine Coon Adoptions

Northern California

mainecoonadoptions.com

Maine Coon Adoptions is a division of SAFE (Saving Animals from Euthanasia). Their volunteers are dedicated to rescuing abandoned, abused, and surrendered Maine Coons and Maine Coon mixes. They work closely with shelters that do not have a no-kill policy and feature on their urgent rescue page Maine Coons that are in danger of being put down.

Books

That Yankee Cat by Marilis Hornidge
Maine Coon Cats: A Complete Pet Owner's Manual by Carol Himsel Daly, DVM and Karen Leigh Davis
The Maine Coon Cat by Joanne Mattern
This Is the Maine Coon Cat by Sharyn Bass

Children's Books

Togus: A Maine Coon Cat Comes Home by Don Carrigan and illustrated by Thomas Block
My Cat, Coon Cat by Sandy Fuller and illustrated by Jeannie Brett
Widget by Clare Newberry
Hurray for Christopher Cat by Virginia Langley and illustrated by Patrick Davis

Articles

"Our Yankee Cat Goes National," by Jane S. Martinke, *Cats* Magazine, July 1969

Web Sites

Dirigo Maine Origin Coon Cats: maine-cooncat.com
Maine Coon Breeders and Fanciers Association: mcbfa.org
The Cat Fanciers Association Maine Coon Cat Breed Council: mainecoonbc.org

ACKNOWLEDGMENTS

After writing this book, I have an even deeper and more abiding affection for the Maine Coon cat and those feelings extend to all the people who have championed and nurtured the breed over the years. I learned so much about this storied cat while researching and writing this book and could not have put it together without the wise words of Marilis Hornidge in her Coon cat bible, *That Yankee Cat.* Through her wit and Yankee forthrightness, I felt a deep kinship. I only wish I could have met her while she was alive. The wonderful

breeders and pet owners whom I interviewed generously shared their love, infectious enthusiasm, and time with me. I am grateful to Beth Kus for her help in editing and for her extensive research, which was invaluable to me as I wrote. Many thanks to Don and Donna Carrigan, Jeannie Brett, Richard and Peggy Wilson, Wanda Cooper, Sasha Laurita and family, Beverly and Zhenya Scott, Kimmy and Duncan Lockie, Barrie Pribyl, Sky Taylor, and Kate Pierce.

Thank you to Michael Steere, who opened the cat door for me, and for his continued support, encouragement, and great editing. The team at Down East has been a joy to work with, especially Lynda Chilton for her incredible design work. Thank you to Terry Bregy, Linda Callahan, Becca Gildred, Sue Smith, and Dawna Hilton.

Thank you to all my friends and family who embody the loyalty, friendliness, affection, and intelligence of the Maine Coon — I am one lucky lady. Meow.